Original title:
The Sea, The Sun, The Tropics

Copyright © 2025 Creative Arts Management OÜ
All rights reserved.

Author: Juliette Kensington
ISBN HARDBACK: 978-1-80581-490-0
ISBN PAPERBACK: 978-1-80581-017-9
ISBN EBOOK: 978-1-80581-490-0

Warm Breezes

A parrot stole my sandwich,
And danced upon my chair.
The gulls are laughing loudly,
As I run about in despair.

Palm trees sway and giggle,
While coconuts drop and bounce.
I try to catch my hat now,
But it rolls away such a pounce!

Island Hues

Bright colors clash in laughter,
As flip-flops make a beat.
The crabs are quite the dancers,
With moves that can't be beat.

A dog chases a beach ball,
And slips right in the drink.
While I'm trying to sunbathe,
They splash me—oh, I stink!

Celestial Play

The clouds are drawn like cartoons,
With faces all aglow.
A dolphin waves hi to us,
As it jumps high and low.

A wig flies off a sunbather,
Gliding through the air.
The seagulls hold a contest,
To see who'll grab the fare!

Wandering Tides

Flip-flops flying left and right,
As waves pull at my toes.
The sand tickles my feet,
Like a playful little prose.

I tried to catch a seagull,
But it snatched my snack instead.
Now I'm stuck here giggling,
While that rascal flies ahead!

Sunset Serenade

In the sky, a melting gob,
A lazy fish gives a subtle bob.
With shades of pink, the clouds all play,
While crabs dance the evening away.

A seagull squawks, a cheeky chap,
Stealing fries from a beachside snack.
Sandy toes and sunburnt nose,
The tide pulls back, and chaos grows.

Lush Getaway

Coconuts fall with a thud and a roll,
While tourists search for the best sun bowl.
Sipping drinks with tiny umbrellas,
We giggle at the bumbling fella.

Palm trees sway, a rhythmic tease,
As locals chase off buzzing bees.
In flip-flops worn and a loud loud laugh,
We try to surf but just take a bath.

Effervescent Oases

A splashy pool with rubber ducks,
While kids make waves and playful clucks.
In hammocks strung between trees so wide,
We snooze and dream, a lazy glide.

Sandy castles rise and then collapse,
While seagulls circle, plotting mishaps.
With fruity drinks and silly straws,
We toast to fun with laughter's cause.

Dreams on the Breeze

Waves clash like a band gone wild,
While beach balls bounce, we laugh and smiled.
The wind whispers secrets just for fun,
Pretending to be the number one.

A hermit crab zooms in a silly race,
Waving goodbye to its old shell place.
With coconut hats flipping like dreams,
We stand amazed at the oddball schemes.

Driftwood Tales

A stick floats by with quite a grin,
Its journeys long, filled with chagrin.
It claims to have met a giant crab,
But mostly drifts where the waves just gab.

We laugh about treasures it might hold,
Like pirate gold, or tales of old.
Yet all we find are seagull stares,
And mysterious scents of ocean flares.

Tropical Auras

Beneath the bright and blazing glow,
A lizard sunbathes, nice and slow.
In a loud hat perched on its head,
It dreams of snacks, not sunburn dread.

While birds complain of the heat's embrace,
A squirrel dons shades, joins the race.
Sipping on smoothies, fruit-filled delight,
They toast to fun beneath the bright.

Horizon's Lullaby

At dusk, the sky spins tales so grand,
A catfish croons with a soft band.
He sings of mermaids, funny and spry,
Who dance with dolphins under the sky.

A fish in a tux, now that's a sight!
Riding waves, full of pure delight.
Sardines clap fins, and turtles twirl,
In this hilarious underwater whirl.

Cascade of Colors

As rainbows spill from the clouds above,
The crabs paint seashells with a shove.
Bubble parties between drifting boats,
Where squids wear bowties and steal the votes.

Bananas float, basking in flare,
A party for fish, without a care.
Jellyfish juggle with goofy grace,
All in good humor, a watery place.

Embrace of Salty Air

With each wave, a splash and smile,
A seagull's joke flies by in style.
Flip-flops dance on sandy shores,
While sunscreen battles the sun's roars.

Crabs in suits march with great flair,
Snatching fries without a care.
A beach ball bounces, darting here,
As laughter drowns out any fear.

Radiant Waterscapes

Waves high-fived the boats so bright,
As snorkels hum a fishy plight.
Flippers flail in clumsy cheer,
And mermaids giggle, drawing near.

The treasure chest filled with lost socks,
Surveys the scene, a paradox.
With every dive, a sploshy dive,
A splashy dance, we come alive!

Beneath the Coconut Canopy

Underneath palms that sway and tease,
A monkey swings with effortless ease.
Coconuts rain like bizarre bombs,
While holiday tunes play out in psalms.

Sunburned tourists chase their hats,
While lizards plot, in winter's chats.
A picnic feast of fruit and cheer,
While ants take orders, serving beer.

Echoes of Tropical Paradise

A conch shell blares a retro song,
As beach-goers groove all day long.
With sunglasses on and spirits high,
They dance like no one's passing by.

A fishing line in chaos tangled,
While dolphins mock the way it dangled.
Chasing shadows, we spin around,
In the rhythm of laughter, joy is found.

Luminous Waters

Splashing around with a splashy sound,
In shimmery waves, where joy is found.
Crabs wearing shades on sandy shores,
Dance with the seagulls, oh what a score!

Rubber duckies float in a race,
While jellyfish do a silly embrace.
Under the glint of a golden delight,
The water's so warm, we'll swim day and night.

Serene Coastlines

Sun loungers line up like a parade,
With umbrellas swaying, a cool charade.
Turtles in hats move slow as can be,
While we sip our drinks, life's a comedy!

Sandcastles guard against the tide's quest,
With flags made of socks, we think we're the best.
Shells in our pockets, and laughter that plays,
Time drips like honey on lazy days.

Fevered Days

The beach is a circus of flip-flops and fun,
With kids playing tag, oh, what a run!
Laughter erupts with each cannonball flop,
As sunscreen warriors attempt to not drop.

Barbecues sizzle with a scent so divine,
Yet bugs and hot dogs can lead to decline.
Between the squeals and the ice cream's delight,
We laugh at the sunburns that boldness incites.

Salt and Shine

Waves come a-rolling, shouting 'What's up?'
While we chase our hats blown off by a pup.
Umbrella fights flare like a starlit brawl,
In this sandy arena, we're having a ball!

The floaties inflate like the mood on the rise,
As seagulls eye snacks with mischievous eyes.
With giggles and splashes, the day's in rewind,
Forever capturing more hilarious times.

Vibrant Shores

Waves crash and tumble, quite the sight,
A crab doing cha-cha, oh what a delight!
Seagulls squawk gossip about the day's fun,
Shells in a conga line, dancing for everyone.

Sandcastle builders wear crowns made of fries,
While sunscreen slathered folks chase tiny flies.
Beach balls bounce high, they fly with a cheer,
Even the sun seems to laugh—what a year!

Celestial Blue

The sky's a big canvas, painted bright and bold,
Where flip-flops and laughter have stories untold.
Ice cream melts fast in the tropical heat,
As bumbling tourists say, "Hey, watch my feet!"

Kids on the shore making mermaids of sand,
A dog steals a hot dog; I simply can't stand.
Flip-flops are flying, a sight to behold,
Under the smile of a sunset turned gold!

Emerald Isles

Palm trees are swaying, like dancers on stage,
With coconuts watching, they just seem to age.
Flipping some burgers while dodging a bee,
Pirates in sunglasses shout, "Come dance with me!"

A hammock is swinging, the nap's never done,
While piña coladas are sipped just for fun.
Laughter erupts as a wave sneaks a peek,
Splashing the folks in their sandcastled peak.

Blissful Retreat

Tanned tourists lounge, with hats far too wide,
While beachside musicians play songs with pride.
Turtles in sunglasses slowly parade,
As cocktails are mixed with a tropical braid.

A game of beach volleyball, full of surprise,
As someone serves hard—confetti in the skies.
Good vibes are contagious, with laughter that flies,
In this playful retreat, where happiness lies.

Heartbeats of the Coast

Waves are laughing, tickling toes,
Seagulls gossip, where the breeze blows.
Sandy castles rise and fall,
Beach ball bounces, what a sprawl!

Flip-flops squeak, they dance around,
Crabby critters scurry to the sound.
Sunscreen battles cheeky rays,
Giggles echo through the bays.

Tanned tourists with drinks in hand,
Trying to dance on soft, warm sand.
Sandwiches spill, laughter explodes,
A feast amidst our sun-kissed codes.

Bikini-clad, a dog jumps high,
Splashing laughter, a playful sigh.
Endless fun, no thoughts of strife,
Just quirky moments, summery life.

Blazing Dusk

Dusk arrives in colors bold,
Ice cream drips, a sight to behold.
Palm trees sway, do the cha-cha,
While hippos dance like they're a star!

Fireflies join the twinkling show,
Kids race to catch them, round they go.
Banana boats spill their flatmates,
Rendering laughter, through giggly states.

Corn on the cob, buttery bliss,
In the glow, not one can miss.
Games of limbo, with a twist,
As we cheer and laugh, we're in the mist.

Underneath a shimmering sky,
Jokes are told with every fry.
The night is young, adventures call,
As we trip on laughter and memories tall.

Swaying Palms

Underneath a leafy hat,
Resting on a sun-warmed mat,
Chasing crabs with tiny feet,
Laughter echoing, oh what a treat.

Sipping drinks with funny straws,
Mixing flavors without a pause,
Dancing with the breeze's tease,
Mimicking the buzzing bees.

Bouncing beach balls in the air,
Dodging waves without a care,
Bikini's tight, but jokes are loose,
Sharing tales, we cut them loose.

As the twilight starts to shine,
We'll toast to each ridiculous line,
With a wink and cheeky grin,
We'll laugh till the day begins again.

Breezy Retreat

In lounge chairs like stars we lay,
Patches of sun, then shades of gray,
Fighting seagulls for our fries,
Their squawks echo as we disguise.

Flip-flops flying, what a sight,
Launching high, a pure delight,
Splashing water, playful glee,
Giggles mixed with salty spree.

The coconut drinks, so whimsically thick,
Slipping through straws, quite the trick,
Sun-hats bobbing like little boats,
Each wave of laughter, the memory gloats.

Sunbathers grumble about the heat,
While we relish this silly retreat,
Today's agenda: smile and play,
Who knew joy could come this way?

Glimmering Shores

Footprints tracing in the sand,
Who'd have thought I'd get caught, unplanned?
Tripping over treasures bright,
Goldfish giggles in the light.

Collective sighs as crabs invade,
Turning our picnic into a raid,
With speckled shells as silly hats,
We pose for photos with goofy spats.

The shell orchestra plays along,
While we dance to the tide's sweet song,
Laughter bubbles, like soda pop,
We'll keep this party going, never stop.

When the day fades into nights,
We'll share our tales of silly fights,
For in this place of sparkling views,
Every moment gives us giggles and clues.

Secrets of the Depths

Diving down with fish in tow,
Surveying secrets we don't know,
Bubbles up like sinking toast,
Underwater giggles, we all boast.

Octopus in fancy shoes,
Testing out his latest moves,
We chuckle as he makes a splash,
Trying hard to form a dash.

Mermaids teasing with their song,
Pulling us where we don't belong,
Waving fins, they jest and jest,
In this watery place, we jest the best.

When the tide levels out the craze,
We'll look back on all our plays,
With salty cheeks and eyes aglow,
We'll remember this afterglow.

Sandy Footprints

In flip-flops I dance, what a sight,
My feet full of sand, oh what a delight!
Seagulls are laughing, they mock my style,
As I trip on a shell and stumble a mile.

Crabs waltz by me, like they've got a plan,
While I wave at a wave as if I can!
Sunburned like a lobster, but I don't care,
I'm out here playing, my worries laid bare.

Timeless Gulfs

The horizon giggles as boats sail by,
I tip my hat to a flipping fish spy.
My drink's a little salty, quite the mix,
I laugh at the umbrellas caught in a fix.

A coconut falls, it's a real knockout,
Palm trees applaud while I twist and shout.
Caught in a moment that tickles my toes,
Each wave is a buddy, my old friend, who knows.

Lunar Tides

The night glows and twinkles, what a scene,
With a moonlit dance, I'm a zany marine.
Crabs are the audience, they clap their claws,
While I show off moves that break all the laws.

The current's my partner, it pulls me around,
I stumble and giggle, I've lost my ground.
Starfish cheer on, in a cosmic parade,
Who knew the night could be such a charade?

Delightful Estuaries

In the bend of the river, my boat takes a twist,
A splash from a gator? Couldn't resist!
With laughter and bubbles, I float on the crest,
While dragonflies whirl like they're on a quest.

The colors are vibrant, like a candy shop,
But I'm stuck in a muck, could it be a flop?
Nature's giggles echo, they dance through the trees,
Reminding me, friends, to laugh with such ease.

Harmonies of Warmth and Waves

In a land where coconuts dance,
Laughter floats in every glance.
Crabs in shorts, they strut with flair,
Sandy feet, no need to care.

Flip-flops flip and seagulls squawk,
Sunburned noses, funny talk.
A cocktail spill, it's quite a sight,
Sipping joy from morn 'til night.

Mango scents in breezy airs,
Tiki masks and silly stares.
Beach balls bouncing, laughter rings,
Together here, we lose our strings.

When the tide just won't behave,
We surf the waves like circus braves.
With joy in heart and sand in hair,
Life's a joke, so come and share!

Legacy of the Gentle Shore

Waves roll in with silly glee,
Shells and crabs hold a jamboree.
The hammock swings, a lazy dream,
Pineapple hats? A fashion theme!

Flip-flops gone, they've run amok,
Buried treasures or sunken sock?
Friends in laughter, drinks in hand,
Every moment feels so grand.

Silly seagulls steal our fries,
As we watch the sunset skies.
Lifeguards wear sunglasses cool,
While kids splash like they're in a pool.

A sunburned back, a goofy smile,
Hats spinning round, let's rest awhile.
Memories made on this soft floor,
We'll laugh again on this gentle shore!

Eternal Waves

Waves giggle as they kiss the sand,
Seagulls swoop in, make a grand stand.
Shells converse with the bobbing tide,
Joy spills over like a fun-filled ride.

Beach balls clash in a friendly fight,
With squawking shouts of pure delight.
Ice cream drips, a sticky fate,
Sandy toes thinking they're first-rate.

Strange floats bob, the sun shines bright,
In this chaos, pure delight.
A toucan's call sounds like a song,
Comedic moments where we belong.

When twilight paints the sky in hues,
We dance to tunes of ocean views.
Life's a play, we're all part of,
Eternal waves, and endless love.

Golden Horizons

On horizons painted bright and gold,
Silly stories often told.
With laughter echoing all around,
Every moment is joy unbound.

Hats flying high like silly kites,
Sandy angels and playful sights.
Crabby contests, who can dance?
Life's a party, take a chance!

Burgers cooking, aroma divine,
Friends throw frisbees, let's unwind.
As waves tickle our suntan skin,
We roll and dance, come join the din.

With bobbing heads and merry cheer,
In this wonder, we find our sphere.
Golden memories, never part,
Each salty breeze will warm our heart.

Harmony of the Elements

Waves dance like a toddler's prance,
With bright rays pulling a silly stance.
Flip-flops flung in the salty spray,
Oh, how they'll never find their way!

Coconuts bob on a frothy ride,
While crabs do disco, with claws open wide.
Seagulls squawk a tune of delight,
As sunbathers giggle in sheer delight!

Beach balls roll like mischief at play,
With all kinds of sunscreen in disarray.
Sandy toes wiggle in pure surprise,
As snacks turn into a food fight arise!

Laughter echoes through the breezy air,
As friends chase kites without a care.
The hammock swings, with an oomph and a sway,
While jellyfish float, just wanting to play!

Environment of Delight

Palm trees sway in a feathery dance,
While beachside umbrellas hold a stance.
Picnics spread on a blanket so wide,
With ants auditioning—what a funny side!

Children giggle, as they make a splash,
While sandcastles crumble in a crash.
Sunscreen globbed, oh what a sight!
Everyone looking like they had a fright!

Morning coffee with a coconut twist,
As locals humorously chant, "Don't miss!"
The surfboard flies, on a rider's mishap,
Creating laughter—a belly flop clap!

The twilight scene brings a whimsical show,
As fireflies join the beachside glow.
Tiny fish dart, in shimmering trails,
As nightfall settles and laughter prevails!

Echoes of the Past

Old buoys bob like grumpy old men,
Reflecting stories from way back when.
Each wave whispers secrets of lore,
As tides recall what they can't ignore.

Nostalgic laughter drifts from the shore,
Where seashells chuckle and crabs implore.
Memories float like a buoy in space,
Time mocks us, playing a funny game of chase!

Worn-out flip-flops tell of past fun,
While sunburns giggle, saying, "We've just begun!"
The soundtrack of waves keeps you on track,
As jokes of the tide take you aback!

Even the seaweed has tales to regale,
Of sailors who told unforgettable tales.
So raise a toast with your fruity drink,
And laugh at the past as we wink and think!

Shimmering Waters

Bubbles rise like giggles in the air,
Fish wearing glasses, quite debonair.
Colorful fins flash as they zoom,
While turtles twirl, trying to bloom!

Surfboards bob, with riders who miss,
Creating splashes—oh, what a bliss!
Look! There's a dolphin, juggling a fish,
Reminding us all to laugh and just wish!

The shorebirds strut in a comical way,
As tourists trip on their beach dayplay.
Sand flies everywhere, what a surprise!
As cheeks turn pink and laughter just flies!

From evening till dawn, let the fun never end,
With stories recited, on laughter we depend.
So grab your pals for a weekend retreat,
In these shimmering waters, life is so sweet!

Caress of Warm Breezes

Warm whispers tickle my cheeks,
As I chase crabs on tiny feet.
Laughter bounces off my flip-flops,
While sunburns dance to my defeat.

Coconut drinks in hand, I sway,
Like palm trees caught in a wild play.
Sand castles leaning to the side,
A royal palace, come what may.

Seagulls squawk with hungry glee,
Stealing fries from my company.
A crab joins in the sandy fight,
This feast is not just for me!

With every wave, I giggle more,
As laughter spills from the shore.
A day of fun, a splashy spree,
Life's wacky choreography for sure!

Tides of Time Unfolding

Waves that swish and swirl in time,
Tickle toes with a playful rhyme.
Seashells giggle, lost in the sand,
Each one's a treasure unplanned.

Sunsets turning everything pink,
Time out here makes you stop and think.
Flip-flops fly as friends partake,
In games of tag by the lake.

Kaleidoscope skies bring out the cheer,
Whispers of fun that all can hear.
With each tide that rolls back in,
More laughter bubbles from within.

As the stars twinkle in the night,
We dance under their twinkling light.
A world of chuckles, bright and fine,
In this sweet place, we all align!

Laughter of Seagulls

Screeching friends with wings so wide,
Dive and dart, carefree they glide.
With snacks in hand, I wave and cheer,
They laugh at my sandwiches, oh dear!

Feathered rascals on the hunt,
Stealing chips, it's a seagull stunt.
I chase them down, yet always fail,
They flap away with a cheeky wail.

High above, the cloud fluff plays,
As we frolic through the sunny rays.
Each peep and squawk fills the air,
A silly chorus, beyond compare.

The beach is bright, the spirits soar,
Every gull adds to the score.
In this playful, breezy banter,
Laughter soars like a bright enchanter!

Sun-Kissed Sandy Dreams

In a world where flip-flops reign,
And jellyfish dance in vain.
Sun-kissed skin, a lopsided tan,
I try to run, but here I stand.

Sandcastles crumble with a laugh,
Each grain a part of nature's craft.
Buckets flying in a sandy race,
Getting stuck in a soggy place.

Tropical drinks with tiny straws,
Sipping slowly, it's worth the pause.
My friends all joke and poke their fun,
This goofy gathering has just begun.

A splash, a squeal, a game of chase,
Time flies in this happy space.
With sunset hues and breezes bright,
We share our silly dreams tonight!

Mirage in Aquamarine

Waves dance like they've had too much rum,
Seagulls squawk, 'Hey buddy, get some!'
Flipping flip-flops, washing ashore,
Who needs a tan? Just find a door!

Shells whisper secrets, give me a giggle,
Lobsters doing a little jiggle.
Crabs pinch and squeal, oh what a sight,
Beach parties start long before night!

Tanned tourists, looking for a spell,
With sunburns that could tell quite a tale.
Pineapple drinks with umbrellas so grand,
Cheers to the fun, we're playing in sand!

But wait – is that a fish wearing a hat?
Swim trunks on dolphins, imagine that!
As laughter rises with each playful splash,
At mirage's edge, we all feel the dash!

A Symphony of Ocean Blues

Waves tickle toes, what a bold trick,
Watermelon smiles – oh, take a pic!
Fish in sunglasses swim with flair,
Shrimp dance like they just don't care.

Beach balls collide, laughter takes flight,
Sunburned games like a slapstick fight.
Sandcastles tumble in a humorous plight,
A royal decree? Hold your towers tight!

Seashells chime like a quirky band,
Starfish waltz with a glittered hand.
Productive crabs with a sassy strut,
Crafting beach puns from each cozy hut!

Waiting for waves to spill forth the crew,
Bikini-clad dreams and a jolly "woohoo!"
A symphony hums, soaked in delight,
As dusk brings a giggle to end the light.

Golden Hour's Serenade

In the glow of orange, crabs sing rock,
While sunbathers snooze, lost in their clock.
Bikini lines sharper than summer's events,
Shadows stretch long, laughter ascents.

Palm trees sway to a breezy beat,
As birds join in, chirping their tweet.
Cocktails spill cheers under twilight's flair,
Who knew that sand could get in your hair?

Shellfish gossip, trading witty lines,
Tilting their heads, sipping on brines.
Sandy feet waltz with a shell in sight,
Golden hour's magic makes everything right!

The horizon blushes with vibrant shades,
As sunset melts and the laughter parades.
A serenade swells, in warm hues it mixes,
Life's a beach, filled with whimsical fixes.

Secrets Beneath the Coral

Bubbles arose from a giggling squid,
"Hey! Underwater shells, please keep it hid!"
Treasure maps made from recycled napkins,
Lead to a kingdom of playful dolphins.

An octopus juggles with flair and grace,
While a blowfish feigns a pufferfish face.
Mermaids toss seaweed like it's confetti,
With fishy jokes that are always ready!

The treasure's just laughter, beneath the blue,
Hidden pearls of wisdom, if only you knew.
As schools of fish form a conga line,
You can't help but chuckle—what a good sign!

Secrets sneak out on a tidal wave breeze,
With playful antics and ample tease.
Under the waves, joy bubbles up free,
In coral's embrace, come swim with me!

Coral Dreams

Beneath the waves, I found a crab,
He wore a hat, which made me stab.
A dancing shrimp, all full of flair,
Said, "Join the party, we don't care!"

A dolphin winked, with quite the grin,
Offered me snacks, I thought, 'How thin!'
A treasure chest, full of old socks,
The pirate's joke, all in knots and blocks!

Starfish clapped, in rhythm they twirled,
While jellyfish glowed, such colors swirled.
I laughed so hard, I lost my kick,
Now I float, quite like a stick!

Here in the depths, where laughter's free,
Who knew the waves could tickle me?
A coral reef, a vibrant scene,
Turns everyday into a funny routine!

Oceanic Embrace

With a splash and a flop, I hit the floor,
A fish yelled, "Hey, you can't be here no more!"
I tripped on sand, it was quite a feat,
Called all my pals, for a raucous retreat!

An octopus danced in polka dot shoes,
Telling old tales of mermaids' blues.
A seagull squawked, "You'd better beware,
I steal your fries, without a care!"

Crabs played tag, in shells all aglow,
While starfish cheered, offering a show.
The surfboard laughed, it's got its own flair,
A true fashionista, like it just don't care!

A conch shell whispered secrets of old,
"I've seen some things that would make you bold."
With each wave, we're caught in a race,
Embraced by giggles, on this sandy base!

Drenched in Light

The rays beat down, I forgot my hat,
While lounging around, next to a cat.
It scratched my toes, said, "Take a break,
The beach is hot, make no mistake!"

A turtle waddled, in quite the chic,
"Let's have a party, don't be so meek!"
He brought a cake, made of seaweed green,
"Best you'll ever taste, if you know what I mean!"

A clam then stuck, out of the sand,
"Mmm, you'll need sunscreen—give me your hand!"
With each fun splash and silly punt,
Drenched in laughter, we made our own front!

With seagulls cawing, we danced a jig,
All while the jelly looked quite the big.
In sandy bliss, with laughter so bright,
Who knew a beach could feel so light?

Tranquil Waters

A floating log called for a chat,
I replied, "Rough day? Living like that?"
It floated, sighed, then gave a wink,
"Chill out, buddy, come have a drink!"

With fish in bow ties, all sipping tea,
They said, "Join us, this is the key!"
A lazy wave rolled, with a big ol' yawn,
Said, "In my embrace, mate, you won't fawn!"

A seahorse jogger, panting with glee,
"Running gets boring, come swim with me!"
Each flip and flop brought bursts of cheer,
Beneath the surface, we had no fear!

With laughter echoing off rippling streams,
Life here is sweet, with all of our dreams.
These tranquil moments, so light and fun,
Are treasures forever, for everyone!

Wandering Souls

On sandy shores where seagulls laugh,
Tourists trip on their own half.
With ice cream falling from their cones,
They dance around like silly stones.

A crab with swagger scuttles by,
In a top hat, oh so spry!
Flip-flops squeak and children squeal,
As waves play hide-and-seek with zeal.

Zephyr's Caress

A gusty breeze steals hats away,
While folks attempt a beach ballet.
Umbrellas fly like kites in flight,
It's quite the show, a comic sight!

Sunbathers snore, sand in their hair,
While dolphins giggle, causing a scare.
The surfboard tips, and off they splash,
With squeals of joy, a wild dash!

Wildflower Waves

Bright blooms sway where the tide will dance,
A bee in shades gives flowers a glance.
Frogs in sunglasses croak a tune,
As waves tickle toes, oh what a boon!

Laughter spills like cocktails on ice,
Each splash a cheer, a wink, a slice.
The picnic spread floats by with flair,
Seagulls dive for snacks, what a scare!

Color-Soaked Skies

Cotton candy clouds drift on by,
As flamingos walk with a sassy cry.
A painter spills colors in the hot air,
While clowns juggle while floating, rare!

The sunsets wear flip-flops with style,
And everyone beams with a goofy smile.
Fishes whisper secrets, who'd believe?
In this wacky world, we all weave!

Paintbrush in the Sky

A giant brush swirls bright and wide,
Clouds giggle as colors collide.
Fluffy sheep dance, oh what a sight,
They argue their shades all day and night.

A flamingo paints with a dab and a splash,
While crabs honk horns, making a clash.
The sky's a canvas of whimsy and cheer,
Where jellyfish float, drinking root beer.

Seagulls critique with their cawing delight,
As rainbows argue about who's most bright.
The balloons in the breeze have a wild soirée,
Sipping on sunshine and playing all day.

A pelican struts, wearing shades of pink,
While turtles groove to the rhythms they think.
With giggles and grins, the horizon's a sight,
Where laughter and color unite day and night.

Sunkissed Retreat

On a lounge chair, a squirrel finds bliss,
Wearing a hat, he can't help but miss.
Cocktails with berries, a curious blend,
He spills his drink on a hermit crab friend.

A monkey swings by with a gleeful screech,
Selling coconuts, a citrusy peach.
Laughter erupts as they barter in jest,
A parade of humor, a zany fest.

Palm trees sway to the rhythm of glee,
While a lobster dances, a sight to see.
Sunbathing crabs take a snooze in a pile,
Snoring in tune, but all with a smile.

With slip 'n slides made of vibrant vines,
Everyone splashes, spilling their fines.
As laughter echoes across sandy bits,
Here fun reigns supreme, in delightful fits.

Tropical Melodies

A parrot croons with a raspy tone,
In a hat made of flowers, sitting alone.
Bongo drums thump as a dolphin prances,
Jellybeans tumble in synchronized dances.

A chorus of frogs sings their bubbly song,
While starfish jam with a boogie so strong.
Guitarists strum on a zany old log,
And even the snails join with a froggy fog.

Turtles tap feet in the rhythm divine,
Swaying their shells, oh, what a fine line!
The sun sets in colors, bedazzling and bold,
As critters unite in this tale to be told.

With giggles of gold, the night comes alive,
Crickets serve punch in the moonlit vibe.
Underneath stars, laughter floats free,
In this symphony of pure jubilee.

Flowing Paradise

A river of giggles flows down the way,
As frogs jump in, splashing bright rays.
They paddle around in children's wide eyes,
On lilypads, telling sunshine lies.

A walrus winks from a dock with a grin,
Inviting the octopus to join in the spin.
With ink blots of humor, the sea critters play,
Creating a carnival, bright as the day.

The breeze carries whispers of jokes in the sky,
As seagulls narrate with a wink and a sigh.
Belly laughs bubble up from the waves,
Echoing brightly in a world that saves.

Fireflies twinkle, firework delight,
While fish throw a party, all trying to bite.
They swirl and they twirl, with joy so profound,
In a flowing paradise where smiles abound.

Whispering Tides

Waves crash and giggle, a silly dance,
Fish wear sunglasses, taking a chance.
Seagulls squawk jokes, with a wink in their eye,
Flip-flops are squeaking, oh my, oh my!

Shells lie in laughter, tickled by sand,
Crabs in tuxedos, just looking so grand.
Dolphins dive down for a playful splash,
While beach balls runaway, oh what a dash!

Sunburned toes giggling in a patch of lush,
Ice cream cones melting, in a sticky rush.
Laughter erupts as kites take a dive,
In this silly paradise, we truly thrive!

A sandcastle crumbles, with kids in a fit,
As laughter erupts, they refuse to admit.
With buckets and shovels, they plot and they plan,
Creating a kingdom, with rockstar flair and tan.

Sunlit Shores

Warm rays tickle noses, what a bright sight,
Turtles in shades lounge, oh what a delight.
Sandy pails giggle, filled with the day's loot,
While flip-flops rebel, they run from their roots.

A crab with a clipboard, counting sea stars,
Winking at kids racing shiny toy cars.
Balloons in the air, at risk to float free,
As chase turns to giggles, wild as can be!

Beach chairs all gossip, in sun-faded talk,
As the cool ocean breeze joins them for a walk.
And umbrellas are dancing, a colorful waltz,
While cooler bags rumble, shouting, "No faults!"

Sunset spills laughter, painting the scene,
A chorus of chuckles, it's simply routine.
With flip-flops in hand, we dance on the shore,
In this comical haven, there's always room for more.

Paradise in Bloom

A garden of giggles, flowers in cheer,
Where bees wear tiny hats, buzzing near.
Palm trees sway joyfully, in vibrant hues,
While pineapples grin, sharing summer views.

The breeze plays tricks with the playful sand,
Kites tangle in laughter, what a grand stand!
Coconuts chuckle, rolling down the way,
While children in swimsuits splash and play.

Bubble baths on waves, soap-sudsy streams,
Shells become trumpets in sunshine dreams.
A hammock hums softly, a tune in the air,
As laughter and sunshine dissolve every care.

With jokes on the horizon, the day's almost done,
As shadows grow longer, our laughter is spun.
In this blooming paradise, joy takes its flight,
Leaving memories of laughter, oh what a delight!

Radiant Horizons

Bright horizons sparkle, like diamonds in line,
While sunburnt clowns juggle, oh what a sign!
Fish wear tiny hats, parading with flair,
And the jellybeans dive, in the salty air.

Children sliding sideways, on doughnuts afloat,
With sunscreen disasters, what comical note!
Beach towels are gossiping, secrets they share,
As waters lie giggling, full of silly flair.

Laughter erupts with each wave that breaks,
Catching the jokes, as the ocean awakes.
Shells with wide smiles, their secrets are bound,
In this funny kingdom, joy always surrounds.

When evening creeps in, with a sky draped in fun,
Laughter lines the waves, as day turns to run.
With sparkling horizons, we dance through the night,
In a place where joy glimmers, oh what a sight!

Blissful Breaches

Waves whisper secrets, oh so bright,
Crabs dance in shoes that fit just right.
Seagulls squawk, they join the show,
While fishies giggle in a splashy flow.

Sandcastles rise, then take a dive,
A toddler's giggle makes the shells thrive.
Lost in a bucket, a flip-flop's plight,
Sunburned toes yell, "That feels just right!"

Palm trees sway, in fancy hats,
A coconut spills, causing belly laughs.
Surfboards wobble, the riders squeal,
Watch the sunburns turn into a meal!

With every splash, joy takes its toll,
As sunscreen dodgers roll out their stroll.
The tide rolls in, and so does glee,
What's not to enjoy in this bright marquee?

Dances with Warmth

A beach ball bounces, oh what a sight,
While sunscreen fights its sticky plight.
Umbrellas twirl like a dance team bold,
As flip-flops slap, their rhythms unfold.

A barbeque sizzles, with a smoky flair,
Hot dogs roll like they don't care.
Sandwiches play hide and seek,
While seagulls plot their bold technique.

Skimboards glide, then hit the shore,
The backflips fail, but laughs galore.
A daring crab takes a speedy run,
Chasing away the afternoon sun.

As the stars peek out, laughter remains,
With tales of wet pants and fishy gains.
Under bright lights, joy shouts and beams,
In the silly dance of vacation dreams!

The Calm Between

In quiet moments, the hues collide,
Waves tickling toes, where legends abide.
A pair of shades, with a funny twist,
Hides the sun's glare while making a list.

Seashells gossip about ocean woes,
"Did you hear? That starfish wears old clothes!"
Fish in tuxedos, oh what a sight,
Paddle by the crabs who party all night.

The breeze tells jokes only palm trees know,
While beach blankets dance in a gentle flow.
Finding conch shells feels like a race,
When a toddler trips, oh what a grace!

Laughter erupts from the ocean floor,
As clumsy dolphins steal the show once more.
A dolphin flops, and everyone sighs,
Just another day, under clear blue skies.

Echoes of Light

Reflections shimmer on a playful spree,
Where sunsets wink, teasing the sea.
A pineapple hat steals quite the glance,
As beachgoers jiggle in a happy dance.

Shells with smiles line the sandy sweet,
Where flip-flops race, oh what a feat!
A fish with shades waves past the pier,
While sunbathers forget their seagull fear.

Ice cream drips, adorned with sprinkles,
As giggles burst in joyful twinkles.
Sand dollars grin, they know the trick,
To turn every moment into a flick.

With laughter echoing on this bright shore,
Even crabs seem to laugh and explore.
In the warm glow, joy rides the waves,
While the sunset paints, and the ocean braves.

Vibrant Threads of Island Life

Bright colors dance on swaying trees,
Laughter echoes with every breeze.
Coconuts drop with a thud and a roll,
As seagulls plot to steal the whole bowl.

Sandy toes and flip-flop flair,
The sunburnt tourists in their bare wear.
Pineapple hats and conch shell phones,
Who knew paradise could feel like home?

Hammocks swing with a creaky tune,
A crab sneaks by, thinks he's immune.
Dancing locals with moves so sly,
Even the fish are laughing, oh my!

So raise a drink, let worries drift,
In this bright place where spirits lift.
With every wave, a new tale to tell,
Life's a beach, and we're under its spell.

Dreams Adrift on Gentle Winds

Whimsical whispers through the palm fronds,
Alligators in sunglasses—who knew they'd respond?
Mango juice rivers and lemonade streams,
Where every sip shatters serious dreams.

Kites dance high, but now faces fall,
The dog's on a mission to steal the ball.
Coconuts giggle as they roll away,
New friends are made in this playful ballet.

The fishermen tell tales taller than masts,
Of fish that could talk and once wore bright hats.
Under the rim of the horizon's glow,
Laughter erupts from each boat in tow.

So let's sail away on a hammock swing,
In a world where we never stop imagining.
From sunsets that twinkle to dustings of sand,
Join the parade, it's silliness unplanned!

Poetry of a Tidal Day

The tide comes in with a cheeky grin,
Waves crash and sprinkle, let the fun begin!
Surfboards line up in a wobbly row,
Each one hoping it's their moment to glow.

Shells hold secrets from creatures afar,
Driftwood stands proudly—a beachside bazaar.
Children squeal and burrow in sand,
Building castles that march to a band.

A dog leaps high at a jellyfish foe,
Declared victory, but we all know,
That wagging tail is quite the charade,
As he retreats with a flip on parade.

So join in the jest, let giggles resound,
In this magical place where joy is found.
Each spray of salt is a child's delight,
Crafting poems of laughter from morning to night.

Colorful Nights Under Starlit Canopies

Underneath twinkling, a parade so loud,
Flipping fish and foot-stomping crowd.
Tiki torches sway while the ukuleles strum,
Everyone's dancing, not one of us glum.

Dinner's a feast, with laughter and cheer,
Where even the crabs think they can steer.
The salsa is spicy, the rhythm's divine,
Watch out for salsa stains—oh, wasn't that mine?

Marshmallows toast with folly and flair,
A squirrel's esteem grows from his daring snare.
Spinach in the dip, who needs that?
We're here for the jokes and a laugh-filled spat!

As the stars wink down on this jolly spree,
Set your sense of humor forever free.
Each chuckle a wave on this joyous night,
In a world where everything feels just right.

Horizon's Melodies

Waves chuckle and play, a dance on the shore,
A seagull who thinks he can sing, what a bore!
Shells gossip with crabs, in the sun's friendly glow,
While beach bums nap, wrapped in dreams, nice and slow.

Flip-flops go flopping, like fish out of the pool,
Kids building castles like they're upstaging fools.
Sand in your sandwich, a taste we don't seek,
But who needs a snack when the laughter's so sweet?

Tanned legs strut proudly, in shorts three sizes too small,
A sunburned dad snorts, while he's making a call.
The ice cream truck's jingle is music divine,
But oh, that sticky mess—sherbet, it's time!

As sun dips away, colors swirl in the sky,
A perfect day ends, but the giggles won't die.
Chasing seagulls as the stars start to peep,
Day's adventures keep us, in joy, rather deep.

Sweet Salinity

Sandy toes dance to a rhythmic façade,
Kids squirt each other, with joy all abroad.
Flipping and floundering, a dolphin-like play,
Beach towels are launching like UFOs in the fray.

Drifting in hammocks while sipping on drinks,
A parrot critiques; well, what does he think?
Lifeguards on towers with visions like kings,
Patrolling the shore like proud eagle wings.

The breeze tells a joke that tickles the palm,
While sunscreen's the combat for heat, oh so warm.
Sandwiches squished flat, like summer's punk rock,
As jelly and chips meet our toes on the dock.

A picnic of laughter, where laughter won't cease,
Digging for treasures, a pearl or a piece.
We'll dance like the crabs in a funny charade,
In this club of the cheerful, we've all got it made!

Journey to Radiance

The horizon is winking, with a grin ever wide,
A trio of dolphins put on quite the ride.
The beach ball's escaping like it's got a degree,
While sun hats fly off in a fierce jubilee.

Picnic ants marching, on a holy crusade,
As ants and the chips have a messy parade.
Sundresses flutter, while all of us smile,
Building new friendships, each moment worthwhile.

Beach volleyball battles, missed hits filled with glee,
Refereed by a mother, she calls out "Just tee!"
Children chasing water; it's a splash zone spree,
And the umbrellas all dance, as if wild and free.

The silhouette laughs, as the sun takes a bow,
An orange and pink soirée, oh wow, look at how!
No worries allowed, just fun's tight embrace,
As day turns to night, we'll all find our place.

Luminous Bliss

Under the twinkling stars, a comet will race,
While party hats float like lost dreams in space.
The surfboards collide, in a slapstick routine,
A gathering of friends, oh, the joy is obscene!

A cocktail of laughter—the kind that won't spill,
Beach parties abound, with a lively goodwill.
Footprints in sand, leading nowhere in haste,
As memories stir up, yet time's never waste.

Coconuts wobble, while drinks create cheers,
With frisbees like UFOs, we cast off our fears.
The playlist of giggles will always remain,
And life's goofy rhythms are hard to contain.

Stars jiggle above as we dance with the tide,
A light-hearted motion, in nature we bide.
Night's gently wrapping its arms all around,
In this luminous bliss, happiness is found!

Nature's Sunlit Canvas

A crab wears a hat, oh what a sight,
Dancing on sand, with all its might.
The seagulls squawk, they join the game,
While sunscreen's on, oh what a shame!

Flip-flops fly as kids run by,
Chasing a kite, oh how it'll fly.
Mermaids swim in pools of giggles,
While waves just chuckle, oh how they wiggle!

The tides are laughing, they tickle the shore,
As beach balls bounce and laughs galore.
Sunburned noses get a cheeky glow,
In this silly place, where joy will flow!

Beneath the palms, the hammocks sway,
As crabs take breaks and dance away.
Nature's palette, what a fun spree,
Painting our hearts with glee, you see!

Journey to Warm Embrace

A mouse with shades is on a roll,
Surfing on waves, fetching a bowl.
Pineapple drinks in hand, so bright,
We toast to mangoes, oh what a sight!

The sandcastles giggle, they tip and sway,
As kids dress shells and join the play.
Frogs wear flip-flops on a lazy day,
Ribbiting laughter, hip-hip-hooray!

With rubber ducks sailing past the fun,
And a crab wearing bling, he shines like the sun.
In this quirky world of sunshine's beam,
Every moment feels like a crazy dream!

A seagull's prank, it swoops and dives,
Stealing chips, oh how it thrives.
We'll giggle and wiggle all through the haze,
In this warm embrace, we're lost in rays!

Ebb and Flow of Radiance

A surfboard's dance, a silly flip,
With sand in toes, we can't help but trip.
Seashells laugh, their stories they share,
While sunburned bunnies forget all care.

The jellyfish jiggle, what a sight to see,
In a wide-brimmed hat, they're fancy and free.
Sand dollars sing, their tunes are sweet,
As we boogie-woogie on our sandy feet!

Palm trees sway, waving to the show,
As shadows stretch long, just like a flow.
The water's charm whispers tales of fun,
As we enjoy this wild run in the sun!

With buckets of laughter, we fill to the brim,
And quirky crabs do a little swim.
Ebb and flow, what a giggle parade,
In a world where silliness will never fade!

Paradise Found at Dusk

As daylight fades, a dance begins,
With fireflies buzzing and cheeky grins.
A crab in a tux, oh, so dapper,
It's the best evening for silly chappers!

The lazy sun dips, paints the scene,
While the breeze whispers, feeling so keen.
Sandy toes shuffle, no worries tonight,
Under a sky ignited so bright.

Piña coladas spill, oh what a spill!
While coconuts cheer, they're never still.
Jellybeans twirl like they own the place,
In this paradise, we dance with grace!

The moon peeks out, with a wink and a smile,
As crabs groove along, in their own style.
Laughter and joy paint a perfect dusk,
In our silly haven, we just must trust!

Tropical Bliss

Sandy feet and laughter loud,
A coconut with a funny crown.
The beach's breeze, a playful tease,
While seagulls dance and tumble down.

Umbrella drinks with tiny straws,
A crab that scuttles like a pro.
Flip-flops flying through the air,
No clue where they might go.

Sunscreen's slippery, oh what fun,
A frisbee flies, but not too far.
Caught by waves with a big splash,
We laugh and forget who we are.

Sandcastles rise, but soon they fall,
With laughter echoing, we stand tall.
For in this place where joy is bound,
We find our bliss, both safe and sound.

Sun-Kissed Sands

A picnic spread upon the shore,
Seagulls eyeing every bite.
A sandwich flies, we laugh and snort,
As chips take their adventurous flight.

Beach balls bouncing, oh so high,
A game of catch? The wind's a witch!
One toss goes wild, another sighs,
And lands with flair - oh what a glitch!

Sandy toes and giggles loud,
A dance-off starts; we twirl and whirl.
With laughter loud, we form a crowd,
As evening sparks a playful swirl.

Then back to blankets, sun sinks low,
Under twinkling stars we row.
With smiles that shine like diamonds bright,
Tomorrow's mischief seems just right.

Azure Reflections

Waves that giggle, splash, and play,
Reflect the sky in a silly way.
A fish jumps up, a playful prank,
At a nearby boat, we've gone out to tank.

Floating floats with laughter loud,
Someone spills - oh, was that you?
Diving deep, we search for fun,
Who knew bubbles stole the view?

Sunnies perched upon our heads,
A tiny crab joins in our stroll.
With every twist, the laughter spreads,
As we race each other, heart and soul.

Evening colors paint the sky,
With all around, we can't deny.
These moments shared, without a care,
Forever bright, a joyful pair.

Sunkissed Serenity

In flip-flops, we chase the tide,
A splash, a scream, a tickled side.
Bright umbrellas sway with pride,
As giggles echo, far and wide.

A sandbank throne, our royal seat,
Where guardians of fun convene.
But watch your drink, it may retreat,
A sneaky wave, so stark and keen!

Shells we gather, treasures new,
With stories tall, we'll weave them true.
A treasure hunt, with friends so dear,
Chasing laughter, that's the queue!

As twilight wraps us in its glow,
With friends surrounding, there's no foe.
Sunkissed paths beneath the stars,
In this funny dance, we are the avatars.

Endless Horizon

A bird on a ball, just taking its flight,
Tripping on clouds, what a curious sight.
Waves laugh at jellybeans dancing around,
While crabs throw a party, all upside down.

Flippers are flapping, the fish have a spree,
A dolphin's in shades, sipping fizzy sweet tea.
Seashells are sunbathing, taking it slow,
While starfish discuss what they really don't know.

A sandcastle tower, a magnificent bluff,
Yelled 'bring me some snacks!' but they just said, 'tough!'
Seagulls are sneaking, a bread roll in claw,
Claiming to be, 'the best since I saw!'

Moonlight giggles when the tide's on a roll,
But don't ask a clam, they'll just mumble and stall.
Here, laughter's the currency, joy is the key,
Now grab a floaty, come splash wild and free!

Dance of Golden Waves

Where the frolicsome swells take extravagant turns,
And sea cucumbers learn the latest new burns.
Pelicans dive with a splash and a grin,
As eager young crabs root for them to win.

Sandcastles wobble as laughter erupts,
While flip-flops and watermelons follow in flubs.
Lemonade fountains, they bubble and sway,
Oh, how the parakeets love their cabaret!

A turtle in shades, sips on coconut bliss,
While tempests of giggles make clouds want to kiss.
A mermaid suggests they just throw a grand fête,
But a sardine sighs, 'Who's going to be late?'

When twilight approaches, the giggles take flight,
As conch shells start singing, and hearts feel so light.
Riding the waves, with a gleeful parade,
Nothing can stop this whimsical charade!

Whispering Shorelines

Waves gossip secrets on the coarse rugged sand,
While flip-flops gossip about someone's bad hand.
Crickets in chorus, a night's silly song,
As lightning bugs host a bash all night long.

A seagull just winked, not sure who to pick,
While shells play charades with a cucumber trick.
The breeze brings in whispers, quite often absurd,
Every wave that returns says, 'Have you heard?'

A beach ball's a hero, rolling with flair,
While a poor little seashell claims, 'Life isn't fair!'
But laughter erupts like the warm summer sun,
In the heart of the coast, where we all get our fun.

So gather your friends, you know the drill well,
It's a carnival chorus where spirits can swell.
Amongst flavors of salt and glimmers of light,
Let's toast to the joy of this humorous night!

Mirage of Distant Isles

A clam proposes to start a new trend,
With shades and a straw hat, he calls it 'The End'.
Parrots all chuckle, with a wink and a strut,
While a crab busts moves in a little pink rut.

Kites swirl and twirl, on a spree of delight,
While children yell 'Jump!', oh what a good sight!
As coconuts bounce and tumble with glee,
Chasing after laughter is a whole jamboree.

The lazy sunflowers dance like they know how,
While snails slide by saying, 'We'll catch up somehow!'
The horizon's on fire with mischief and jest,
As we raise our shell cocktails, this trip is the best!

So let the balmy breezes carry us far,
To places where giggles become every star.
In the mirage of fun that stretches out wide,
We're here for the laughter, come join for the ride!

Island Reverie

On a hammock, I take a nap,
Dreaming of my next big snack.
Coconut drinks, oh what a treat,
It's hard to move with my sandy feet.

Seagulls squawk, a noisy crowd,
Stealing fries, they're oh-so-proud.
Children play, splashing with glee,
While I dodge their water spree.

My sunhat flies, it's in the breeze,
Chasing it feels like a tease.
Flip-flops squeak as I take a stand,
Life's a joke on this sandy land.

But as I laugh, I trip and fall,
A belly flop, oh what a call!
Laughter echoes, hearts collide,
In this paradise, I cannot hide.

Whispering Palms

Coconut trees sway, shaking heads,
I swear they gossip under spreads.
"Who wore those shorts?" they smirk with glee,
"The brightest colors we ever did see!"

Crabs in their shells, tapping their feet,
Having a dance-off, what a treat!
One let out a sneeze, oh what a blast,
The other just laughed, 'You're an outcast!'

Bikinis are bright, quite a sight,
One lady's top gave an unexpected flight.
The palm trees snicker, the waves chuckle,
Even the tide giggles, oh what a shuffle!

Flip that towel, let's start a game,
Is this a beach or a circus fame?
With jokes and jests, the fun never ends,
Sandy laughter, where joy transcends.

Currents of Joy

Waves roll in with a splash and a dash,
While I'm busy finding my last snack stash.
A surfboard tumbles, oh what a sight,
I think I'll just stick to daydreams tonight.

The rooster crows, a wake-up alarm,
But all I want is to find some charm.
Sipping pineapple, feeling so swell,
But I dropped it—guess I'll just dwell.

Fish flip-flop like they're in a dance,
While I fling my arms, trying to prance.
"Catch me if you can!" they wave and tease,
But I'm just here enjoying the breeze.

Sunsets paint the sky all bright,
Shades on my eyes, what a sight!
As darkness falls, I shall not fret,
For tomorrow brings more laughs, you bet!

Fading Light

As daylight dims, here comes the show,
Crabs put on hats, stealing the glow.
Dancing shadows on the beach,
With a limbo game just out of reach.

Fireflies flicker, a glowstick race,
"Catch me if you can!" they leave no trace.
A banana boat tips, oh what a scene,
Riders tumble, looking quite mean!

The last rays tease, play hide and seek,
But laughter echoes, it's joy we speak.
Who knew the night could be so bright?
In this quirky paradise, all feels right.

So here I'll stay, in twilight's embrace,
With silly plans, let's join the chase.
As we bid adieu to this playful land,
I'll wrap up joy like it's made of sand.

Reflections on Crystal Waters

Waves dance like silly children,
Splashing laughter on the shore.
Flip-flops fly in wild abandon,
What's that? Oh, a sandy chore!

Sunshine burns with a goofy grin,
While seagulls plot their next heist.
Can you believe it? Fish wink back,
'Catch us if you dare, you sliced your rice!'

Umbrella drinks with tiny umbrellas,
Sipping joy under the blaring heat.
Every sip's a tropical giggle,
While sun-kissed toes tap to the beat.

Shells tell tales of parties past,
Where crabs danced like they won a race.
Under every rock, a secret waits,
An ancient clam? Nah, just a face!

Chasing the Horizon's Light

Flip through your shades, what do you see?
A mystery wrapped in sunset hues.
Surfboards zoom like caffeinated bees,
While jellyfish watch our every move!

Skimboarding dreams on slippery tar,
Every wipeout's a comedic delight.
Pull up a coconut, beneath the stars,
And stumble over laughter, with all your might.

Palm trees swaying, doing the twist,
They're the party hosts of this sandy spree.
As shoreside musicians make a hit,
Sorry, neighbors, this jam is free!

So grab your hat, let's hit the road,
Every selfie a meme, pure gold,
Play hide and seek with flamingos neat,
Before the tide reveals the jester's fold!

Serene Escape to Bliss

Coconuts singing on a warm, soft breeze,
Laughter floats like dandelion seeds.
Chasing crabs with clever antics,
Watch your toes—an escape artist's tricks!

A pineapple party's happening near,
With squishy fruit, a taste of cheer.
Ants in line for their picnic feast,
What a crazy, little gathering, to say the least!

Tropical shirts, oh what a sight,
Stripes and polka dots hit the light.
Snorkeling? More like kick and stumble,
Who knew fish could be so humble?

As the twilight wraps us in a hug,
The stars giggle like old-time friends.
Snuggle up tight for the cosmic tug,
Tonight, every worry just pretends!

Breath of the Ocean's Heart

What's that in the distance? A sense of whimsy,
A treasure hunt led by a crab so tricky.
Seashells chime with tales so silly,
Each one a giggle, not too picky!

Surfboards stacked in a wobbly tower,
Marooned in sun, not a hint of dour.
Naps on the beach? Oh, what a power,
Till the sunburn laughs at your hour!

Kites tumble down like happy clowns,
Twisting and turning in the gentle air.
Who knew they could wear such frowns?
The limbo dance? Just why we dare!

Sandy footprints tell a story, so grand,
Of beach ball battles and splashy plays.
As the tide rolls in, it surely will stand,
A comedy show in salty praise!

www.ingramcontent.com/pod-product-compliance
Lightning Source LLC
Chambersburg PA
CBHW072215070526
44585CB00015B/1345